AGAINST THE ODDS

Stephen Hawking

Cath Senker

raintree

a Capstone company — publishers for children

Raintree is an imprint of Capstone Global Library Limited, a company incorporated in England and Wales having its registered office at 7 Pilgrim Street, London EC4V 6LB – Registered company number: 6695582

www.raintreepublishers.co.uk
myorders@raintreepublishers.co.uk

Edited by Linda Staniford and Jennifer Besel
Designed by Philippa Jenkins and Tim Bond
Picture research by Tracy Cummins
Production by Helen McCreath
Originated by Capstone Global Library Limited
Printed and bound in China by LEO

ISBN 978 1 406 29754 6
19 18 17 16 15
10 9 8 7 6 5 4 3 2 1

British Library Cataloguing in Publication Data
A full catalogue record for this book is available from the British Library.

Acknowledgements
We would like to thank the following for permission to reproduce photographs: Alamy: Art Directors & TRIP, 27, ZUMA Press, Inc, 22; Corbis: Bettmann, 11, Hulton-Deutsch Collection, 14, REUTERS, 30, Roger Ressmeyer, 19; Dreamstime: Smartin69, 13; Everett Collection: Liam Daniel/Focus Features, 41, Rex Features, 40; Getty Images: Bob Mahoney/The LIFE Images Collection, 17, Brand X Pictures, 20, BRUNO FAHY/AFP, 33, Chip Somodevilla, 37, David Levenson, 15, 42, David Montgomery, 25, Ian Waldie, 39, JIM WATSON/AFP, 34, Jonathan Brady, 38, LEON NEAL/AFP, 4, National Geographic/James A. Sugar, 31, Terry Smith/The LIFE Images Collection, 26; Homer Sykes: My British Archive, 24; Landov: Reuters, 28; Magnum Photos: Ian Berry, 18; NASA: 35, JPL-Caltech, 43; Newscom: UPI Photo/Kevin Dietsch, Cover; Rex USA: 6, 8, 10; Science Source: Mike Werner, 29, Richard Kail, 36; Shutterstock: banderlog, 16; Wikimedia: A. T. Service, 23, MRC National Institute for Medical Research, 12, Wikimedia /National Institute of Standards and Technology, 9.

We would like to thank the following for permission to reproduce quoted text:
pp5, 21, 25, 27 Reproduced by kind permission of John Gribbin and Michael White taken from the book "Stephen Hawking: A Life in Science" by Michael White and John Gribbin (Penguin, 1992); p31 Excerpt(s) from MY BRIEF HISTORY by Stephen Hawking, copyright © 2013 by Stephen W. Hawking. Used by permission of Bantam Books, an imprint of Random House, a division of Random House LLC and by permission of The Random House Group Ltd. All rights reserved; p43 ©Professor Stephen W. Hawking from speech given to Cedars-Sinai Regenerative Medicine Institute, Los Angeles, April 2013.

Contents

Some words are shown in bold, **like this**. You can find out what they mean by looking in the glossary.

Who is Stephen Hawking?

Stephen Hawking greets the
audience at the opening ceremony
of the London 2012 Paralympics.

It is the opening ceremony of the 2012 Paralympic Games in London. Stephen Hawking, probably the most famous living scientist, wheels on to the stage. Watched by millions of viewers around the globe, he launches the event, to the ecstatic cheers of the crowd.

Hawking is known worldwide for his great contribution to **cosmology** – the scientific study of the origin of the **universe**. Just as importantly, he has encouraged the general public to take an interest in science.

Success against the odds

Hawking's success as a scientist – and indeed his very survival – are against all the odds. When he was 21, he was told he had two years to live. Yet 50 years on, he still goes to work every day at Cambridge University, helping **PhD** students, discussing ideas with staff and students, and working on his own theories. Sometimes he is interrupted by a visit from a famous person, such as former astronaut Buzz Aldrin, one of the first men on the moon.

Stephen Hawking was a talented student at Oxford University, one of the United Kingdom's top universities. He continued his studies at Cambridge University and became a cosmologist. Hawking made important discoveries about **black holes** in space and developed a new way of working in cosmology.

Hawking's biographers, Michael White and John Gribbin, have written that:

"He has achieved astounding success by awakening a sceptical [doubtful] public and an even more sceptical media to the beauty of science, a subject at the heart of our society and the future of civilization."

5

What was Stephen Hawking's childhood like?

Stephen was the first baby born to Frank and Isobel Hawking, on 8 January 1942. His parents had both attended Oxford University, although it was unusual to go to university in the 1930s, especially for women. After they left university, his father became an expert in tropical diseases, while, like most women in those days, his mother brought up the family.

Here is Stephen Hawking as a schoolboy with his younger sisters, Mary and Philippa.

Who's who

Dikran Tahta

(1928–2006)

Stephen was inspired by Dikran Tahta, his maths teacher at St Alban's school. Tahta encouraged his students to think creatively about their subject and take part in lively discussions. He later became a mathematics teacher at Exeter University.

A family of thinkers

Stephen had two younger sisters, Mary and Philippa, and an adopted brother called Edward. Frank and Isobel gave their children plenty of freedom. The house was full of books, and the family talked freely about all kinds of subjects. Other people thought the Hawkings were rather odd. They went on holiday in a brightly painted wooden gypsy caravan pulled by a horse, and once drove to India in an old Ford Consul car.

As a child, Stephen loved making things. When Frank made Mary a doll's house, Stephen put in plumbing and lighting. As he later explained, he had a "passion to understand how things worked – from toy trains to the universe". Young Stephen often gazed at the sky for hours.

At the age of 11, he passed an exam that allowed him to go to a **grammar school**, and he started as a pupil at St Alban's school, near London.

7

A teenage scientist

As a teenager, Stephen's interest in science grew, and he filled his bedroom with metal and wire gadgets. He wasn't interested in rock 'n' roll music like many other young people. Instead, he and his friends enjoyed reading, making complicated board games, going on long bike rides and attending classical music concerts.

This photo shows Stephen enjoying boating in the 1950s – a hobby he would later take up at university.

This is an early computer: the operating console is in the middle, and the tubes containing the memory are right behind it.

While Stephen was studying for his A levels (secondary school leaving exams) in maths, physics and chemistry, he built two computers from scratch with his friends, using clock parts and bits of a telephone switchboard. They called it the Logical Uniselector Computing Engine (LUCE). It solved logical problems — "if this condition is true, then another thing will happen". Years later, the school's Head of Computing found a box of junk and threw it away. He had no idea it held Hawking's computer.

Science student

When he was 17, Stephen took some tough exams and won a place at Oxford University to study science, focusing on physics. At the time, he found physics boring because it was so simple for him, but he felt that "physics and **astronomy** offered the hope of understanding where we came from and why we are here."

COMPUTERS

In the 1950s, just a few computers existed in universities for scientific research. They were huge, sometimes taking up an entire room. A small group of trained experts used them for complicated maths problems. No ordinary person could operate a computer — you needed to be able to write computer programs.

9

Off to university

In 1959, after taking his A Levels, Stephen went straight to Oxford University. He found the course easy, so he was rather lazy. He later worked out that he had spent an average of one hour a day studying during his three-year course!

He made the most of university social life though, acting as the coxswain (the person who steers the boat) for a rowing team. The boat club enjoyed lively parties, too.

Stephen Hawking was the cox for the Cambridge University rowing team, seen here in 1961.

Albert Einstein
(1879–1955)

Stephen Hawking based his work on Albert Einstein's theories. Before Einstein, people thought that measurements of time and space (the distance between objects), together known as "**space-time**", were the same all over the universe. Einstein realized that they are different if the people measuring are moving at different speeds. He worked out that the **gravity** (pull) of the Sun bends light, so space-time is curved – similar to the way a blanket dips if you hold the corners and throw a ball into the middle.

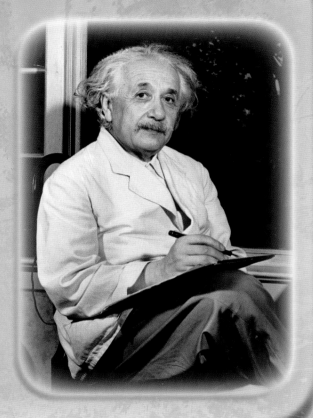

Cosmology at Cambridge

Although he hadn't worked hard, Stephen managed to achieve a First – a top degree – and decided to do a PhD in cosmology at Cambridge University. **Astronomer** Dennis Sciama was his **supervisor**.

At the time, exciting debates about the universe were raging. Britain's best-known astronomer, Fred Hoyle, believed in the Steady State theory: the universe had always existed and would exist forever. But another idea had emerged. The Big Bang theory suggested that the universe had started with an initial **expansion**. Stephen was keen to explore this new idea.

How did Stephen Hawking become a professional scientist?

During his last year at Oxford, Stephen had grown clumsy, and once he fell down the stairs. He went to the doctor, who simply told him to stop drinking beer.

Just after starting his PhD in 1962, Stephen went home at Christmas. He went skating on a frozen lake, fell over and couldn't get up. His parents took him to London for medical tests, and 21-year-old Stephen was shocked to discover he had Amyotrophic Lateral Sclerosis (ALS) – known as motor neurone disease in the United Kingdom and Lou Gehrig's disease in the United States. Stephen was told he had only two years to live.

Amyotrophic Lateral Sclerosis (ALS)

ALS kills the nerve cells in the brain and spine that allow people to move their muscles. Over time, a person with ALS is unable to use most of the muscles in his or her body, but the disease does not affect the brain. There is no cure. Only 10 per cent of people with ALS survive for more than 10 years.

Frank Hawking had urged his son to study at Oxford or Cambridge University. He and the rest of the family were devastated when they found out about Stephen's illness.

This is Gonville and Caius College, Cambridge. Hawking joined the college in 1962 and is still based there today.

Making the most of life

At first, Stephen felt depressed, spending a lot of time in his room listening to extremely loud classical music by Wagner. But then he started to snap out of it. Whenever he felt miserable, he remembered the boy opposite him in hospital who had died of leukaemia (blood cancer), and realized some people suffered more than him. With the threat of death hanging over him, he decided to work as hard as possible in the time he had left.

Professor Fred Hoyle was a creative scientist who was not afraid to come up with new ideas.

The will to live

Stephen found another reason to live when he met Jane Wilde, a girl who was living and studying in St Albans. Their relationship developed even though she knew how ill he was. Jane visited at the weekends to enjoy picnics by the river and relaxed trips in punts (flat-bottomed boats) with Stephen and his friends. The couple got **engaged** in 1964.

In the early 1960s, Stephen was studying at the Department of Applied Maths and Theoretical Physics (DAMTP), a new institute in Cambridge. Now he was engaged, he became even more motivated to work hard. He was eager to complete his PhD, find a job and marry Jane.

Jane Hawking
(born 1944)

Jane Wilde married Stephen Hawking despite his serious illness. Her Christian faith helped her to cope with caring for her husband and bringing up three young children (see page 18). She later returned to her own studies, did a PhD and became a teacher. Jane has written two books about her life with Stephen.

Taking on Fred Hoyle

In 1964, Stephen Hawking indicated that he was already a scientist to be reckoned with. He knew that Fred Hoyle was planning to give a talk about the Steady State theory to the Royal Society, a group of important scientists. Hawking managed to sneak a look at Hoyle's paper beforehand and made calculations that showed some mistakes in the paper. At the meeting in London, he told Hoyle he was wrong. Hoyle was furious!

The Big Bang theory

Stephen Hawking was convinced that Hoyle was wrong, and that the Big Bang theory was the key to the beginning of the universe. Most scientists didn't believe it because if there had been a Big Bang, how was it created? Did this idea mean that there was a creator God?

Hawking looked at the theory of black holes for clues. A black hole has such strong gravity that it pulls in everything, even light. At the time, mathematician Roger Penrose was investigating how a black hole forms when a star dies. The force of its own gravity makes it collapse into one extremely **dense** point, which Penrose called a **singularity** – the centre of a black hole.

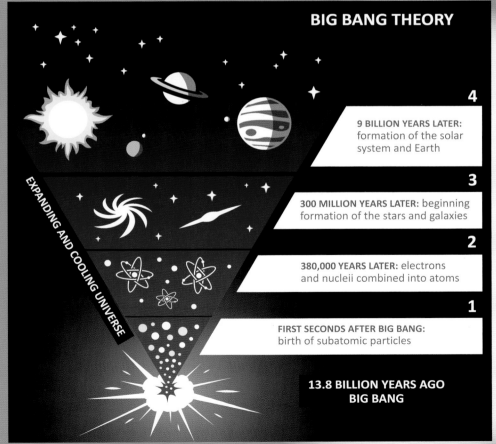

BIG BANG THEORY

4

9 BILLION YEARS LATER: formation of the solar system and Earth

3

300 MILLION YEARS LATER: beginning formation of the stars and galaxies

2

380,000 YEARS LATER: electrons and nucleii combined into atoms

1

FIRST SECONDS AFTER BIG BANG: birth of subatomic particles

13.8 BILLION YEARS AGO BIG BANG

EXPANDING AND COOLING UNIVERSE

This illustration shows how the universe came about, according to the now widely accepted Big Bang theory.

Roger Penrose
(born 1931)

Mathematician Roger Penrose worked out many of the features of black holes. In 1969, along with Stephen Hawking, he proved that all the material in a black hole collapses to a singularity – a point of infinite (limitless) density. It's like squeezing a massive object such as the Sun to the size of a dot, and continuing to squeeze forever.

The start of the universe

One night, travelling back to Cambridge with other scientists, Stephen Hawking had a flash of inspiration. What if the reverse of Penrose's theory had happened in the Big Bang? Perhaps the universe had started as a black hole and then expanded. Hawking didn't think God was needed for this process to occur – the Big Bang could have happened on its own. Now he worked intensely on this idea for his PhD.

How did Stephen Hawking's career take off?

Hawking completed his PhD and applied successfully for a post at Cambridge University. Knowing he had a job, he and Jane got married in July 1965. For part of their honeymoon, they attended a physics conference in the United States. Jane realized she would be sharing her husband with the world of physics.

Home life

The Hawkings soon started a family: Robert was born in 1967 and Lucy came along three years later. Stephen was delighted and played as much as he could with the children. In the late 1960s, when he had to start using a wheelchair, he used to play tag with Robert and Lucy, wheeling around the garden after them.

Stephen Hawking enjoys a relaxing moment with his family, 1977.

Amazingly, Hawking had survived far longer than the doctors predicted, but his disabilities were increasing. He began to lose the use of his hands so that he couldn't write easily. He adapted his working methods, learning to do much of his work in his head.

The scientists Penzias and Wilson, seen here in 1993, used this radio telescope to discover microwave radiation in space.

MICROWAVE RADIATION

In 1965, scientists Arno Penzias and Robert Wilson discovered **microwave radiation** in space. This radiation wasn't caused by any interference – it didn't even come from our **galaxy**. They knew that if there had been a Big Bang, there would be low-level radiation in the universe now. This discovery helped to prove Hawking's argument that the universe had a beginning.

Stephen Hawking explains that if you fell into a black hole you'd be stretched out as thin as spaghetti, which he calls "spaghettification"!

The mysteries of black holes

One evening in 1970, it suddenly occurred to Hawking that when two black holes collide and merge, the surface area of the new black hole is greater than the areas of the two black holes put together. Hawking suggested this might be linked to the area of physics called thermodynamics, the study of heat and movement. This new discovery made Hawking famous in the world of cosmology.

A shock for the scientists

Hawking made his next major discovery in 1974. At the time, most scientists believed that nothing could escape from a black hole. But Hawking found that black holes can give off **radiation** – in the same way that a hot body gives off heat. This meant that a black hole could shrink and eventually disappear once all the radiation had escaped.

When Hawking announced his findings to a cosmology conference in February 1974, the audience was shocked. Instead of thanking Hawking, the chairman remarked that his theory was preposterous. But later Hawking was proved right, and the escaping radiation was named Hawking Radiation.

In the same year, the science community recognized Hawking's talents and elected him Fellow of the Royal Society, a great honour. At 32, he was one of the youngest-ever members.

Hawking's biographers described what happened soon after he announced his theory about radiation escaping from black holes:

"... physicists all over the world were discussing his work.... Some physicists went so far as to say that the new findings constituted [formed] the most significant development in theoretical physics for years."

A year in California

In 1974, the Hawking family had the opportunity to spend a year in sunny California, USA, so that Stephen could work at the California Institute of Technology (Caltech). He was treated like royalty – he was offered a high salary, a large, comfortable home, an electric wheelchair and an office with all the adaptations he needed for his disability.

In the 1970s, Caltech was a top institute for theoretical physics.

Seeking black holes

Hawking was keen to work with Kip Thorne, a well-known theoretical physicist. He had a bet with Kip that the **two-star system** Cygnus X-1 didn't contain a black hole. He really wanted to lose the bet because he wanted to discover a black hole. But if he won, he would at least enjoy his prize, a subscription to the political magazine *Private Eye*. Eventually, in 1990, he lost the bet because Cygnus X-1 was proved to be a black hole.

While in California, Hawking lost the use of his hands, but he was able to work out **equations** and picture the universe in his head, and he developed an extraordinary memory.

Who's who

Kip Thorne
(born 1940)

At Caltech, Kip Thorne headed the group working on the nature of space, time and gravity, building on Einstein's theories. He also researched black holes. In the 1980s, he wrote about the idea of **wormholes** – tunnels between two points in space-time that could make time travel possible. As yet, there is no evidence that wormholes exist.

Science for everyone

The Hawkings returned to England in 1975. They now had a comfortable ground-floor apartment in a large house, with gardens where the children could play.

Here is Stephen Hawking with Jane and their children, in Cambridge, 1981.

Professor and popular writer

In 1979, Jane gave birth to their third child, Tim. That year, Hawking became Lucasian **Professor** of Maths, a senior position at Cambridge University. However, **academic** life rarely brings riches, so Hawking decided to write a science book aimed at ordinary people. He needed money to send his children to private schools and he wanted millions of readers to discover cosmology. He began work on his book, *A Brief History of Time*, in the early 1980s.

It was a tremendous job for Hawking to write about physics in a way that ordinary readers could understand.

US publishing company Bantam was sure the book would be a hit and offered Hawking a large sum of money. His **editor**, Peter Guzzardi, worked hard to simplify the book for general readers and persuaded Hawking to leave out his equations.

In 1985, while Hawking was writing, he fell seriously ill and nearly died. He had an operation on his windpipe so that he could breathe but it meant that he could no longer speak at all. Would this end his career?

Jane Hawking decided Stephen should have the windpipe operation but she wondered whether it was right to take away her husband's ability to speak:

"The future looked very, very bleak. We didn't know how we were going to survive – or if he was going to survive."

How did Stephen Hawking attract global attention?

Hawking now needed constant care from nurses. He could only communicate by raising his eyebrow when someone pointed to the right letter. In this way he slowly spelled out words.

Walt Woltosz, a computer expert in California, heard about Hawking's difficulties and developed a special computer for him. The screen had rows of letters at the top and rows of words at the bottom; Hawking could select words by pressing a switch. In Cambridge, David Mason linked the computer to a speech **synthesizer** so that Hawking could talk using an artificial voice.

This is Stephen Hawking in 1988 – the computer Woltosz created for him is attached to his wheelchair.

A surprise success

These gadgets allowed Hawking to carry on working, and *A Brief History of Time* was published in 1988. The publishers were amazed and delighted – the book was on *The New York Times* bestseller list for 147 weeks and the British *Times* bestseller list for a record-breaking 237 weeks. It was translated into 40 languages and to date has sold more than 10 million copies.

Although many people found the book too difficult to read, Hawking received lots of letters from readers asking questions or making comments about it, and cosmology became a popular topic of conversation. He became famous worldwide, going on chat shows and even appearing on *Star Trek*, his favourite science-fiction show.

This is the cover of Stephen Hawking's book. He believed the book's success showed that people have a deep fascination about how the universe works.

Stephen Hawking wanted *A Brief History of Time* to reach a wide audience:

"I am pleased a book on science competes with the memoirs of pop stars. Maybe there is still hope for the human race. I am very pleased for it to reach the general public, not just academics."

Crises and cosmology

Stephen Hawking loved the media attention for his book and was thrilled that ordinary people were interested in cosmology. But the press started to pry into his illness and family life, which was a great strain for Jane. The couple drifted apart; they separated in 1990 and later divorced.

Marriage to Elaine

In 1995, Hawking married again. His new wife, Elaine Mason, had been one of his nurses. They had spent a great deal of time together and grown close. It proved lucky that he was married to a nurse – Elaine saved Stephen's life on several occasions.

Stephen Hawking with his bride Elaine at their wedding. Her ex-husband David had designed Hawking's speech synthesizer.

Thomas Hertog
(born 1975)

Top-class Belgian scientist Thomas Hertog took his PhD at Cambridge University, supervised by Stephen Hawking. He has worked on cosmology and string theory: the idea that all the **particles** in the universe are made up of tiny, wobbling strings – rather like guitar strings. They are so tiny that scientists can't see them even with the most powerful microscope.

This is a computer artwork showing what the strings in string theory might look like.

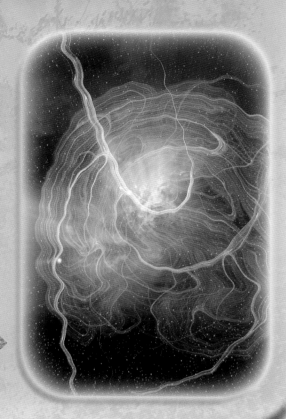

Top-down cosmology

Against the odds, Hawking survived crises like these, and his scientific work thrived. In 2006, he worked with Thomas Hertog to develop a new way of working in cosmology. Usually, cosmologists took a maths model – a set of equations – and used it to predict the state of the system at a point in the future. Hawking and Hertog invented top-down cosmology. They decided to start with the universe as it is today and work backwards to find out what it was like in the past.

Life as a celebrity

In 2007, Stephen and Elaine divorced – his reliance on her to look after him made the relationship difficult. From then on, he lived at home with carers to support him. In 2009, he retired as Professor of Maths because he was 67, and all Lucasian professors had to retire at that age. But he continued to go to work, and his life certainly didn't slow down.

Stephen Hawking met former South African president Nelson Mandela on a trip to South Africa in 2008.

Living with fame

At the start of the 21st century, Stephen Hawking is a true celebrity, often attending events with famous people and giving lectures to packed audiences. He is possibly the best-known scientist in the world. But sometimes Hawking wonders how much of his fame is because of his science and how much is because of his disability.

There are some drawbacks to being well known. He can't do everyday tasks such as going shopping without people rushing up to him to take photographs, and the media constantly pry into his private life. Yet he feels the good aspects of fame outweigh the bad.

Stephen Hawking has remarked on how his disability has actually helped him in his academic work:

"In some ways I guess it has been an asset [benefit]: I haven't had to lecture or teach undergraduates [degree students], and I haven't had to sit on tedious [boring] and time-consuming committees."

Regardless of his fame, Hawking continues to spend much of his time engaging in debates about scientific theories.

Criticism and controversy

Stephen Hawking's work has sometimes led to **controversy**. That's normal in science – when you come up with a new idea, people often resist it. Hawking has often been proved right in the end. For example, his findings in 1974 showing that black holes give out radiation were seen as ridiculous at the time. Further research then showed Hawking was correct, and by the late 1970s, the theory was widely accepted. Now, it is seen as a breakthrough in theoretical physics.

No space for God

Hawking's view of the creation of the universe is still disputed though. He believes that the universe grew from nothing, which leaves no room for the idea that God created the world. This theory goes against religious views of how God created the universe. People of faith regularly send him letters arguing with his views. In Hawking's opinion, his critics get upset for no reason – he is simply stating his scientific discoveries and others are free to decide if they believe them or not.

TIME TRAVEL

Hawking says time travel is impossible. If it were, surely we'd have seen tourists visiting from the future! He believes that somewhere out there, **alien** life forms exist. But he warns against sending out messages to other worlds in case hostile aliens find out about us and decide to invade. However, many other scientists think it's important to send messages into space to show that there is life on Earth.

So many students turned up for Hawking's lecture at Leuven University, Belgium in 2011 that the university decided to put up a giant screen so that all 2,500 students could watch.

What has Stephen Hawking achieved?

In 2008, Hawking and his daughter Lucy gave a lecture called "Why we should go into space".

At a personal level, Stephen Hawking's achievements are extraordinary. Whenever his disease has grown worse, he has adapted his working methods. One secretary who worked for him was amazed when he dictated 40 pages of equations from memory. The following day, he remembered a mistake he'd made! With such an incredible memory, he can work things out by turning them over in his mind without needing to write anything down.

Against the odds, Hawking has had a family life and his own children have done well. For example, Robert studied physics at Cambridge like his father and then went to work in the United States. Lucy studied at Oxford and became a successful journalist.

World traveller

Nothing has stopped Stephen Hawking from living life to the full. He loves parties, and has always had lots of people coming for dinner and discussions at his home. Hawking has travelled the world – he has visited every continent, including Antarctica. He has even been on a zero-gravity flight, where he floated as people do in space, and down in the ocean in a submarine. Hawking hopes one day to travel into space.

Here is Hawking on a zero-gravity flight, where he was able to float free from his wheelchair.

www.goZeroG.com

This is a computer image of a black hole, with matter falling into it. The flash shows escaping Hawking Radiation.

Science achievements and awards

Stephen Hawking has had an impressive scientific career, working with the world's leading scientists to come up with some of the ideas physicists currently use in their work. He challenged the Steady State theory of the universe and helped to make the Big Bang theory popular, which is now accepted as the theory of how our universe began.

He helped to develop the theory of black holes in the 1960s, long before anyone knew they actually existed – the first black hole was identified in 1990. Hawking also worked on the top-down model for thinking about the universe, which other cosmologists have adopted.

Awards

Hawking has received a host of awards for his scientific work, including the Fundamental Physics Prize in 2012, awarded for his work on black holes and Big Bang cosmology. He has received awards from the Queen of England and a Medal of Freedom from US President Barack Obama.

MAKING HAWKING RADIATION

It's impossible to travel to a black hole to test if Hawking Radiation definitely exists. But in 2014, scientists at the Technion-Israel Institute of Technology in Haifa, Israel, set up an experiment in the lab and created a very similar effect to Hawking Radiation.

US President Barack Obama presented the Medal of Freedom to Hawking in 2009. The Medal of Freedom is the highest American honour for a civilian (someone not in the military).

Fighting for fairness

Stephen Hawking is not shy about putting forward his views, and he is outspoken about the rights of disabled people. He has successfully campaigned in Cambridge to make it easier for disabled people to access museums, libraries and theatres, and he supports charities that help people with physical disabilities, especially motor neurone disease.

Helping those in need

Hawking is a champion of fairness. He has spoken out about poverty in the United Kingdom and to defend the **National Health Service**, without which he wouldn't be alive. In 2014, he supported Save the Children's campaign to help Syrian children suffering in the country's civil war, voicing their pleas for help in an advert.

Hawking met Queen Elizabeth II at an event held by Leonard Cheshire Disabillity, a leading charity supporting disabled people.

Stephen Hawking opposed British involvement in the war in Iraq of 2003 and joined an anti-war rally to read out the names of war dead in 2004.

Spending on science

Hawking stands up for the importance of science to society. In 2010, he criticized UK government cuts to university funding, which he believes are holding back progress in science. Yet he does not support all scientific developments – he is opposed to **nuclear weapons** because of their devastating effects.

ASSISTED SUICIDE

Stephen Hawking takes an active role in the debate over assisted suicide – helping people with an **incurable** disease to die. In 2006, he argued that assisted suicide was wrong, but he changed his mind. In 2013, he said he thought that those in terrible pain with no hope of a cure should have the right to end their lives, as long as it is clearly their decision.

A popular scientist

Many scientists are barely known outside their academic field but Stephen Hawking is quite the opposite. He has enjoyed being part of popular culture, writing science books and appearing in newspapers and TV shows.

Comedy appearances

Hawking has a great sense of humour. He has made guest appearances on the US cartoon show *The Simpsons*. In 2003, he featured in a comedy sketch on the TV show *Late Night with Conan O'Brien* in which he spoke on the phone to actor Jim Carrey. Hawking told Carrey and O'Brien not to bother discussing cosmology "because their pea brains cannot possibly grasp the concept".

Jim Carrey and Stephen Hawking struck up a friendship, and the actor visited Hawking at his home in Cambridge in 2003.

A huge audience

On a more serious note, Hawking gives public lectures about cosmology around the world. In 2010, 5,500 people attended a talk in London – his ideas were so complex that many could not follow what he was saying, but they were pleased to hear such a great man.

Several buildings have been named after Hawking, including the Stephen Hawking Building, a teaching centre at his college in Cambridge. There's a Stephen Hawking Centre in Ontario, Canada and a Stephen W. Hawking Auditorium in Texas, too.

This is a still from the film *The Theory of Everything*, which was based on Jane Wilde's 2004 book about her life with Stephen Hawking.

FILM AND TV

Hawking has been involved in several films. In 2004, British actor Benedict Cumberbatch played him in the TV movie *Hawking*. In 2010, Hawking wrote a documentary series called *Into the Universe with Stephen Hawking*, and he featured in a documentary about his life in 2013. *The Theory of Everything*, a film about his relationship with Jane Wilde, came out in 2014.

How is Stephen Hawking's work continued today?

Stephen Hawking loves to discuss ideas with PhD students and colleagues, and he's had an enormous influence on the next generation of physicists. His former students, such as Fay Dowker, Gary Gibbons and Raymond Laflamme, are all researching aspects of cosmology.

Hawking's work has inspired other scientists to communicate their ideas to the public, encouraging ordinary people to take an interest in physics. For example, Brian Cox and Jim Al-Khalili in the United Kingdom, and Neil deGrasse Tyson in the United States, have featured in popular science programmes about the nature of the universe. Brian Cox is excellent at explaining tricky scientific ideas to the public, often through simple experiments. Such efforts can spark interest and lead to more young people studying physics.

In 2011, Brian Cox appeared at the Hay Festival of Literature and Arts, UK, to explain that the laws of gravity, time, matter and energy are the same throughout the universe.

On a negative note, Hawking strongly believes that we are causing so much damage to the Earth that the future of the human race lies outside our planet. **NASA** is planning to send a manned mission to Mars within the next 20 years, so perhaps Hawking will be proved right once again.

Stephen Hawking believes that:

"Mankind will not be able to live a thousand years, if it doesn't find other planets as a new place of residence. We must continue to go into space for humanity. We won't survive another 1,000 years without escaping our fragile planet."

This is an artist's idea of a vehicle that will test out landing technologies for future missions to Mars.

Timeline

1942
Stephen Hawking is born in Oxford on 8 January

1959
Hawking goes to Oxford University to study science, specializing in physics

1962
Hawking starts his PhD at Cambridge University

1963
Hawking is diagnosed with Amyotrophic Lateral Sclerosis (ALS)

1965
Hawking marries Jane Wilde

1970
Hawking makes an important discovery about black holes that makes him famous in the world of cosmology

1974
Hawking discovers that black holes can give off radiation. He is elected Fellow of the Royal Society. The Hawkings go to California for a year.

1979
Hawking becomes Lucasian Professor of Maths at Cambridge University

1988
A Brief History of Time is published and rapidly becomes a bestseller

1990
The first black hole, Cygnus X-1, is identified

1995
Hawking divorces his wife Jane and later the same year, he marries Elaine Mason

2006
Hawking and Thomas Hertog invent top-down cosmology as a way to work out what the universe was like in the past

2007
Stephen Hawking and Elaine Mason divorce

2009
Hawking retires as Lucasian Professor of Maths

2012
Stephen Hawking launches the 2012 Paralympic Games in London

2013
Hawking features in a documentary about his life

Glossary

academic to do with education, especially studying in schools and universities

alien creature from another planet

astronomer person who studies objects in space

astronomy scientific study of the Sun, Moon, stars, planets and other objects in space

black hole area in space that nothing, not even light, can escape from, because gravity (the force that pulls objects in space towards each other) is so strong there

controversy public argument about something that many people strongly disagree about

cosmology scientific study of how the universe started and how it changes over time

dense heavy in relation to its size. For example, a wooden brick is denser than a balloon.

editor person who checks and corrects a book before it is published

engaged when a couple agree to marry

equation statement showing that two amounts or values are equal. For example, 2x = 6 (when x = 3).

expansion process of getting bigger

galaxy large system of stars with their planets. Our galaxy is the Milky Way and contains the Sun and eight planets, including Earth.

grammar school secondary school for young people in the UK who pass special exams in their last year of primary school in order to attend

gravity force that pulls objects in space towards each other. For example, gravity pulls the Moon towards the Earth so it orbits the Earth rather than shooting off into space.

incurable a disease that cannot be cured is said to be incurable

microwave radiation radiation that fills the whole universe and is left over from the Big Bang at the start of the universe

NASA US government organization that carries out research into space and space exploration

National Health Service public health service in Britain that provides medical care and is paid for by taxes

nuclear weapon extremely powerful weapon using nuclear energy; one nuclear bomb can kill thousands of people immediately

particle very tiny piece of matter, the substance that everything in the universe is made of

PhD abbreviation for Doctor of Philosophy – the highest level of university degree. A PhD student has to do their own research into a subject.

professor university teacher of the highest level

radiation heat or energy that is sent out in the form of heat or rays

singularity point at the centre of a black hole that is infinitely dense

space-time three dimensions of space – length, width and depth – plus time, making four dimensions altogether

supervisor person in charge of a PhD student at university, who offers them advice and helps them with their work

synthesizer electronic machine for making sounds

two-star system Solar System with two stars, unlike our Solar System, which has one star, the Sun, with planets moving around it

universe whole of space and everything in it, including the Earth, all the planets and all the stars

wormhole possible link between regions of space-time that are far apart. If it was possible to go through a wormhole, you could time-travel.

Find out more

Books

George's Secret Key to the Universe, Lucy and Stephen Hawking (Corgi Childrens, 2008)

Stephen Hawking, Sonya Newland (Wayland, 2015)

Websites

www.bbc.co.uk/history/people/stephen_hawking
This website has highlights from BBC programmes about Stephen Hawking.

www.esa.int/esaKIDSen/StoryoftheUniverse.html
This website explores the story of the universe, with links to other websites on the universe, the Big Bang and the birth of galaxies.

http://spaceplace.nasa.gov/black-hole-rescue/en
This NASA website for younger readers is about black holes.

DVDs

Into the Universe with Stephen Hawking (Discovery Channel, 2013)

Stephen Hawking's Universe (GoEntertain, 2011)

Through the Wormhole with Morgan Freeman (Discovery Channel, 2014)

Places to visit

The Science Museum
Exhibition Road, South Kensington, London SW7 2DD
www.sciencemuseum.org.uk

Visit the Cosmos and Culture section of the Museum to find out more about cosmology.

The National Space Centre
Exploration Drive, Leicester LE4 5NS
www.spacecentre.co.uk

Visit the National Space Centre to find out more about the universe.

Index